THE FACTS ON
SPIRIT
GUIDES

John Ankerberg
& John Weldon

HARVEST HOUSE PUBLISHERS
Eugene, Oregon 97402

Other books by
John Ankerberg
and John Weldon

The Facts on Astrology
The Facts on False Teaching in the Church
The Facts on the New Age Movement
The Facts on "The Last Temptation of Christ"
The Facts on Jehovah's Witnesses

THE FACTS ON SPIRIT GUIDES

Copyright © 1988 by Harvest House Publishers
Eugene, Oregon 97402

ISBN 0-89081-713-8

Printed in the United States of America.

CONTENTS

SECTION V—A Modern Illustration of Channeled Revelations: The Religion of Eckankar

SECTION VI—An Analysis and Critique of Channeling

About This Booklet

This booklet discusses a subject of great relevance. This is the increasingly popular phenomenon of what may be termed voluntary spirit-possession or "channeling." Channelers claim a spirit actually enters their body and speaks as a "guide" through them. The key issue is this: Exactly who or what are these spirit guides?

Many ideas, even bizarre ones, have been considered. Are they merely the hallucinations of the mentally unstable, as doctors say? Are they parts of the unconscious mind available to us all, as some psychologists say? Are they creatures from the future, or are they from civilizations deep in space, as some scientists say? Are they reflections of a divine aspect to man—a "higher" Self that is now emerging as part of a dramatic leap in humankind's spiritual evolution, as some ministers say? Are they genuine spirit beings such as angels, the dead, or the "gods" and nature spirits of various religious traditions, as the channelers say?

Or are they another category of being entirely—the demons mentioned in the Bible?

The biblical view is rarely examined by those who study psychic phenomena. Parapsychologist (one who scientifically studies the occult) Alan Gauld refuses even to discuss the theory of demons because he says it is "now so rarely put forward that I shall nowhere consider it.[1] Those involved in studying channeling might be expected to have a natural bias against believing in the demon theory because it would implicate them with a view scorned by their associates.

Nevertheless, if one looks for a theory to explain all the facts, the demon theory cannot be ignored, whether or not it is personally appealing. Even William James, one of the great pioneers of Western psychology, once stated during his own investigations into channeling (then termed "mediumism"):

> The refusal of modern "enlightenment" to
> treat "possession" as a hypothesis to be spoken
> of as even possible, in spite of the massive

human tradition based on concrete human experience in its favor, has always seemed to me a curious example of the power of fashion in things "scientific." That the demon-theory ... [i.e., evil spirits] will have its innings again is to my mind absolutely certain. One has to be "scientific" indeed to be blind and ignorant enough to suspect no such possibility.[2]

Again, if there is even a slight possibility these spirits are demons, the reader should be concerned. If it is probable they are such, the question of involvement with them is settled. We invite the reader to examine the logical evidence which has caused many others with us to conclude that the spirits of channeling are not who they claim.

Section I

Channeling: An Introduction

1. What is channeling?

"Channeling" is a "New Age" term for spirit-possession. This occurs when humans willingly give their minds and bodies to spirit beings. These spirits enter and control people and use them to give spiritual teachings or other information. When spirits use the mouth and speak out information, this is called channeling.

2. How popular is channeling in America and around the world?

In America there are thousands of channelers. Millions of followers seek out the channelers for advice or read the literature given by the spirits through their channelers.[3] Based on the sales of channeled literature, tapes, and seminars, channeling in America is a hundred-million dollar a year enterprise.[4] Some have referred to America's growing interest in channeling as having "epidemic" proportions.

If we consider this phenomenon historically, we may understand the potential and dangers of channeling to shape our future. For example, in 1851 there were an estimated 1,200 mediums in Cincinnati, Ohio alone, as well as hundreds of mediums in other major cities.[5] By 1855, America boasted several thousand mediums and some 2 million followers.[6] These channelers and their followers undergirded an entire century of parapsychological research (the scientific study of the occult) in our country.[7] This research, in turn, helped to pave the way for the modern occult explosion.[8]

Today, Los Angeles is estimated to have about 1,000 channelers[9], indicating that we are at the beginning stages of another revival of interest. But the spirits today are turning to highly-sophisticated marketing techniques through radio, television and video.[10] In addition, the endorsement of channeling by famous television and movie stars is making the practice socially acceptable. Examples of stars who have this kind of influence are Shirley MacLaine, Linda Evans (of "Dynasty"), Michael York (of "Romeo and Juliet") and others.[11]

Actress Sharon Gless, who plays "Cagney" on the hit TV series "Cagney and Lacey," won a 1987 "Emmy" for her role on the series. In her acceptance speech, she told tens of millions that her success was due to "Lazaris," a spirit-entity who speaks through medium Jach Pursel.

The popularity of channeling can also be seen through new retreat centers and workshops around the country. In both, people are taught how to open their minds and bodies to the spirits to become channels themselves. In these retreat centers and workshops, live teaching sessions are taught by the spirits themselves, motivating people to start study groups, research centers and magazines devoted solely to the study or development of channeling.[12]

Another area showing the popularity of channeling is its growing influence in the sciences and other disciplines. The spirits are speaking out of their human hosts, giving information which is applied to theories in psychology, to the practice of medicine, to the investigation of parapsychology, to the study of physics, to the application of sociology, and to the development of new ideas in theology, archaeology, and other disciplines.[13] In New York, spiritism has been used for several years as an adjunct to psychotherapy in some New York community mental health centers.[13a]

Not only in America is channeling popular, there is an increasingly visible channeling movement emerging throughout the Western World, including Canada, England and West Germany.[14] Brazil boasts over 1 million channelers or spiritists of various types with millions of followers.[15] All in all it is safe to say that the influence of spirits speaking out of people will be with us for decades to come and its fruits will affect the lives of our children.

3. Why is an ancient occult practice so exciting and attractive to modern twentieth century Americans, including even skeptics?

People today have a great need to find meaning in life. They have discovered, often painfully, that it cannot be found in a material view of reality alone. Even skeptics desire to know the answers to questions like, "Who am I?" "Why am I here?" and "What happens when I die?" Whether or not they admit it, the thought of life being no more than a few years of pain and pleasure replaced by eternal nonexistence is frightening to people. Men know they are more than the end product of hydrogen atoms and blind chance. And they are clearly searching for answers.

Modern man sees channeling as the proof of the deeper answers to life. Channeling seems to answer questions about the nature of reality (Is it spiritual?), the nature of death (Is it the end?), the nature of human potential (Is it unlimited?), and the nature of the self (Is it divine?). Thus, channeling powerfully persuades by claiming access to the very spirit world which can provide answers. The spirits are giving information which deceives men into thinking they are in contact with men who once lived on the earth, who died and who now exist happily in the afterlife. The spirits claim that through death they have found the answers to life and the knowledge that all men will live forever. The spirits claim to speak with certainty about the nature of God, the purpose of life and about what happens at death. They claim there is no Hell and that God and Heaven are not as the Bible has stated.

Channeling thus provides a false answer to modern man's need for religious experience. He is deceived into thinking such contact with the spirits gives meaning to his life and soothes his fears of death.

Think for a moment about what races through the mind of a person powerfully confronted by spiritism. It is like a blind person who suddenly is given his sight. Instantly, all is changed as he sees a new world of great wonder waiting to be explored. Likewise, the person encountering what he believes are genuine spirits of the dead believes death is no longer the end, the moment of absolute loss, but merely the beginning of a joyous new existence of literally unlimited possibilities.

People are deceived into thinking there is no Hell to worry over, only the unending potential for advancement. The spirits do more than persuade; they exert great power over both the minds and hearts of men. This is the appeal of channeling.

4. Who are the channelers?

Channelers come from all walks of life. They include clerks and scholars, artists and businessmen, truck drivers and Ph.D.'s, scientists and grade school dropouts, business executives and housewives. They come from all races, nationalities, cultures and creeds. Some are atheists (initially); others are religious. Except when in a trance and possessed, they look and act normally.

Channelers often channel more than one spirit. Well-known channelers and their main spirit guides include Jane Roberts and "Seth." "Seth," through Roberts, has produced around 25 different books, which together have sold millions of copies. Another channeler was Helen Schucman. Schucman and her spirit guide "Jesus" are the author of the best-selling *A Course in Miracles*. Another channeler is Ruth Montgomery. Her spirit guide is "Lilly." They have written numerous best-sellers on New Age topics. Another is Kevin Ryerson and his spirit guide "John," one of actress Shirley MacLaine's favorite channelers.[16] Ryerson is one of the more articulate channelers and has appeared on dozens of radio and TV shows. On these shows he offers live interviews with his spirit guides.[17] Another channeler is J. Z. Knight who channels "Ramtha." Knight claims she is a former Fundamentalist Christian. Knight has sold almost a thousand hours of "Ramtha's" video and audio tapes. Like many channelers, she is now a multi-millionaire.[18] Another channeler is Jach Pursel who channels "Lazaris." He runs a multi-million-dollar corporation entitled "Concept-Synergy." This corporation is dedicated to making Lazaris' teachings available to thousands of other people.[19] Lazaris' teachings have been especially popular among Hollywood movie stars.[20] But Lazaris' influence is not restricted to Hollywood. Amazingly, such diverse groups as Mennonites, Mormons and Catholic nuns also testify to their following Lazaris' teachings.[21] (In Question 14 we briefly examine the religious views of some of these spirits.)

5. What evidence would lead thinking people to conclude channeling isn't all fraud and fantasy?

Many converging lines of evidence suggest the reality of another dimension of spirits who may be contacted by the proper occult methods. First, the belief in spirit contact is universal. It has occurred in all countries of the world throughout human history. This is documented by a great body of research. One study of nearly 500 modern societies revealed that seventy-four percent accepted the reality of not just spirit contact but of actual spirit-possession.[22] Something must account for so universal a belief. The skeptic who claims that such spirits do not exist holds his view in spite of this evidence.

Secondly, all major world religions have taught the reality of a spirit world. For example, Hinduism, Buddhism, Christianity and Islam all believe in a world of good and evil spirits that may interact with men.[23]

Thirdly, possessed people during channeling are able to give knowledge of the future and describe events taking place in another room or on the other side of the world. In other words, they exhibit knowledge, power and abilities which they do not have when they are not in a trance.[24]

Fourthly, exorcism cannot be adequately explained without assuming the reality of possessing spirits. Jesus Christ Himself believed in the reality of a dimension of demonic spirits and personally cast them out of individuals.[25]

All of this is evidence for the reality of spirits.

6. Why does it matter who or what these "spirits" are as long as they help people?

Discovering their identity is vital. If they are evil beings, then even their "helping" is a deception. No matter what we think of them, it will change neither their nature nor their goals. If we view them incorrectly, we will be deceived by them. To misidentify a poisonous snake as a rope may be deadly. Thus, how we view these spirits is important. It is our interpretation as to their nature that will determine our personal response to them. If they are delusions, we will seek to help those suffering from them with medical assistance. If they are part of the unconscious mind or human potential, they will be sought out by those desiring to explore the powers of the mind. If they are angels or other benevolent spirits, or the human dead, they will be sought out for their spiritual wisdom or insights into life's great mysteries. Indeed, if these spirits really are highly-advanced beings or the human dead, there is no reason not to seek their wisdom, for they may prove a genuine boon to human welfare. This is the standard argument. Nevertheless, if they are demons and irretrievably evil, to seek them out is foolish. Those who do so would sooner or later become their victims. Thus, identifying exactly what is happening in channeling is essential. For example, the fins of both sharks and dolphins are similar. What at first appears to be a playful dolphin could in reality be a deadly shark. To play in the water when only fins are visible could prove fatal.

7. Should people trust the spirits speaking through channelers?

First of all, it must be stated there are both fake and real channelers. For example, in Q. 26 we discuss channeler M. Lamar Keene who was a fake pretending to channel the dead to make money. But it is interesting to note that many occultists such as channelers, shamans, psychics, mediums, and gurus have testified to the fact the spirits sometimes have deceived them. These occultists say the spirits imitate good spirits but actually trick, lie to or injure their hosts. Occultists have found the spirits can imitate virtually anyone or anything with ease. Thus, Satprem, a disciple of occultist and Hindu guru Sri Aurobindo, states what all occultists know—that the spirits "can take all the forms they wish."[26]

The harrowing experience of astral traveler Robert Monroe is typical. In one of his many out-of-the-body experiences, he relates that he was repeatedly and viciously attacked by evil spirits. At one point in the fray, two of them instantly turned into exact images of his two daughters, emotionally throwing him off balance in his fight against them.[27] If occultists testify that the spirits have deceived them and that the spirits take different forms and they have taken these different forms for evil purposes, then it only seems reasonable that the spirits should not be trusted.

Another example of this is the famous medium Emanuel Swedenborg. He spent an entire lifetime associating with spirits. In the Western world perhaps no one else has had more experience with the spirit world than he. Yet Swedenborg cautioned that these spirits were so cunning and deceitful that it was almost impossible to determine their true nature. As an occult authority Swedenborg warned people that the demonic spirits are gifted actors and routinely imitate the dead. Thus, in a frightening way Swedenborg continues to caution people by saying,

> "When spirits begin to speak with a man, he ought to beware that he believes nothing whatever from them; for they say almost anything. Things are fabricated by them, and they lie. ... they would tell so many lies and indeed with solemn affirmation that a man would be astonished.... if a man listens and believes they press on, and deceive, and seduce in [many] ways.... Let men beware therefore [and not believe them]."[28]

Unfortunately, despite all his cautions, Swedenborg himself fell prey to deceiving spirits by thinking his God had given him permission to contact the spirit world. Swedenborg ignored God's warning in Scripture against all forms of spirit contact (Deuteronomy 18:9-12). The reason Swedenborg ignored God's warning is that he believed "good" spirits had taught him the truth. Yet the "church" Swedenborg founded as a result of these "good" spirits has ever since promoted spiritistic revelation that is among the most anti-biblical and anti-Christian material ever printed.[29]

So, can spirits speaking through channelers be trusted? If evil spirits do exist, and occultists tell us it is impossible for them to distinguish the good spirits from the evil ones, who is safe? They need some objective standard by which to test them. Channelers admit they do not have an objective standard. Therefore, their trust in the spirits is blind. Furthermore, if these spirits are demons, they could mask their evil intent for years and no one would be the wiser.

The Bible teaches that is exactly what is happening (II Corinthians 11:14; I Timothy 4:1). In many cases the true goal of the spirits is to give false teachings, the consequences of which are learned too late or fearfully realized after death (Proverbs 16:25; Matthew 24:24; John 8:24,44; Galatians 1:6-8; I John 4:1; Revelation 16:14).

Even bad men succeed in masking their true intentions to deceive others. We may cite Jim Jones as an illustration. Rev. Jones made many claims to being a minister of God. He was engaged in numerous "good works" through his church. But all along many signs were present that something was seriously wrong with Mr. Jones. Authoritarianism, intimidation of others, physical abuse of children, and irrational acts existed side-by-side with the "good." But Jones had power and charisma. He had an "explanation" for the evils and the failures. As a result many chose to ignore the warning signs and to believe he really was a good man sent of God. The end result was tragedy for over 900 people. The same type of situation exists with the spirits. They claim to be good. They claim to be representatives of God. But the warning signs are there.

Is it impossible to think that spirits could never mask their true intentions, like Jones? Yet in occult cases that have been researched, red flags have appeared (for those willing to see them) showing that the spirits' natures are evil. Even doing their best to imitate good, these spirits appear to have a difficult time suppressing their desires to harm men. Perhaps this is why the spiritists themselves sometimes suspect the motives of their contacts. Anyone reading what occultists say will conclude the fact that the spirits bring as much pain and suffering into their host's life as they may safely explain away. The spirits are master psychologists with long experience in dealing with human nature. The spirits know what they can get away with and how to cover their tracks. And the spirits have been doing it for thousands of years. People who would never trust a stranger are trusting strange spirits by the thousands. Yet there are dozens of points of similarity between spiritism (or channeling) on the one hand and the phenomena of demonism on the other. This includes the demonism of China, India, Japan and other countries as well as the demonism of the Bible.[29a] Thus, those who trust the spirits do so even though the entire history of spiritism is littered with evidence that these beings are demons.

Section II

The Characteristics and World View of Channeling

8. What happens during channeling?

When a channeler goes into a full trance, it is as if he is falling backwards into a deep sleep. Both his facial muscles and lips twitch as the invading spirit begins to gain control over the person. Once the spirit is in possession of the body, changes in breathing occur and the person's facial features and expressions are different, sometimes greatly different (for example, the late Jane Roberts). What can be most noticeable is when the voice changes; for example, a feminine voice becomes deep and masculine.[30]

The person who is possessed by the spirits may describe it as similar to an alcohol blackout or to what occurs in hypnosis. The person loses consciousness. Later he awakens. He is told he has said and done things he would not normally have done—yet he remembers absolutely nothing. He is told there was a total takeover of his individual personality. He became like a puppet under the control of a greater power.

Full trance-channeling may involve anything that is normally done in the body, from writing to painting, to singing and dancing, to composing music, to counseling or teaching others.[31]

There are two basic kinds of channeling—intentional and spontaneous. In "intentional" channeling the person actively seeks to be possessed by the spirits. And the spirits usually wait for that person's permission to enter the body. On the other hand, in "spontaneous" channeling the spirits simply take control when they please. The channel is at their mercy. Yet even intentional channels may suddenly find themselves at the mercy of their formerly polite spirit guides.[32]

Channeling can involve different forms; for example, one form may involve complete loss of consciousness and another may involve partial loss of consciousness. Thus, there is full trance-possession with total loss of consciousness, and light-to-moderate trance-possession, in which the chan-

14

neler retains full or partial awareness of his surroundings. In addition there is " sleep" channeling where the spirits teach or influence mediums during their sleep or in their dreams. Another form is known as "automatism" where the spirit seems only to control part of the body such as the hands in automatic writing or painting. There is "clairaudient" channeling where the medium only hears the words dictated by the spirits. There is "clairvoyant" channeling where the spirits put certain images, pictures or symbols into the mind of the person. There is also what is termed "physical" channeling where the spirit uses the medium to affect or alter the environment. For example, the spirits either through a medium or on their own may materialize images of dead people (called "ectoplasmic manifestations"); they may move or levitate objects or imprint them with messages or pictures, or they may transfer objects from one location to another (known as teleportation).[33]

Remember, it is clear that whatever power the medium uses comes only as a result of his contact with the possessing spirit. It is universally recognized that apart from these spirits, the channelers have no power.[34]

9. How are people used by the spirits to become channelers?

Once the proper "invitation" is given, a spirit may unexpectedly take over a person at any time. There are no rules. Millions today are giving out such invitations ignorantly, with little idea of just who may arrive. One of the easiest ways to encounter the spirits or to be possessed by them is to deliberately seek altered states of consciousness. There are hundreds of such methods, including drugs, meditation, yoga, and hypnosis.[35] Channeling is also developed by direct contact with the spirit world through Ouija boards[36] and attending seances.[37]

10. Who do the spirits claim they are?

The spirits claim to be many things. Judging from their own teachings, by far the most common assertion is that they are the spirits of the human dead. A recent prestigious poll revealed that over 40 percent of all American adults— approaching half the nation—claim to have been in contact with someone who has died. Of these, 78 percent claimed they saw, 50 percent heard, and 18 percent claimed to have talked with the dead.[38] From this it is clear the spirits most often claim they are human spirits who have survived phys ical death. They also claim they can reveal important information to men that will hasten their spiritual growth. Further, the spirits claim they are more evolved than we are because they have lived through many lifetimes and discovered the secrets of life and death. The spirits claim that if enough people will listen to them, they can even help to bring a worldwide spiritual awakening. This will produce a New Age of peace and harmony.[39]

We should also keep in mind that the spirits will also appear in the form most desirable or interesting to the one they are seeking to contact. For example, the spirits claim to be extraterrestrials (including Martians and Venusians), various gods of ancient or modern cultures (or God Himself), Jesus Christ, ascended masters, "group beings," angels and nature spirits. By doing this, they know they will spark the interest of the people they are contacting. They may also claim to be various aspects of the human mind or the "collective" mind of humanity (some of the terms used here include the Creative Unconscious, the Higher Self, the Oversoul, the Super-conscious Mind, the Universal Mind, and the Collective Unconscious). They also claim to be the Holy Spirit, troubled ghosts, the spirits of animals and plants (dolphins, trees, flowers), multiple human personalities, the inhabitants of mythical cultures (Atlanteans, Lemurians), and even a possible alien computer that exists in the future.[40] Critics, realizing that some people are claiming to channel dolphins, others the spirits of fruits and vegetables and still others computers from the future, have come to conclude the sanity of the nation is at risk.

11. What possible reason would "spirits" have for imitating the dead?

The Bible tells us there are such things as "unclean spirits" or demons. These spirits are so evil they will never be redeemed: these spirits already know they will eventually be consigned forever to a place Jesus called Hell (Matthew 8:29). The Scriptures lead us to conclude the real motive of the spirits is to take as many men to Hell with them as possible by preventing their salvation (John 8:44; II Corinthians 11:3,4,13,14; Hebrews 2:14; I Peter 5:8). If these spirits really are the human dead, then men can only conclude the dead are free to roam and, therefore, God has not judged them at the moment of death as the Bible teaches (Luke 16:19-31; Hebrews 9:27; II Peter 2:9). If, as the spirits say, the dead are not judged, then human sin is not an offense to God requiring separation from Him (Isaiah 59:2). If sin does not separate man from God, then Christ did not have to die for man's sin (I Peter 2:24; I John 2:2). According to the spirits' views, this means man's faith in Christ as Savior from sin is unnecessary (John 3:16). And if men never trust Christ and receive Him as their Savior, then at death they go to judgment and the demons have achieved their goal (II Thessalonians 1:8-10). To help them deceive men, the spirits enthusiastically teach what their presence as the dead implies—they teach there is no judgment and Christ did not die for our sin. In fact, these demons teach that all men are divine and as such do not even require salvation. The only things they recommend are minor adjustments in man's thinking. In this way the spirits have tricked men into rejecting what the Bible teaches about God, Christ, the death of Christ, man's sinful condition, the necessity of his salvation and final judgment and Hell.

12. Why are spirits contacting men?

They claim they are here to help us. Most spirits claim to be the human dead. They claim they have come back to convince men not to fear their eventual death. Because the spirits say they are just normal men who have died, they claim they can offer us the truth about what will happen when men die.

They also claim they are here to enlighten us spiritually. They say that the purpose of life is to realize our true divine nature—that we are God. The spirits teach that the cause of humanity's problems is really ignorance of its divine nature, not human sin. They say that men need to accept the fact that they are part of God if human problems are ever to be solved. Beliefs like salvation, sin, guilt and judgment are worn out concepts, and according to the spirits, must be discarded. The spirits promise there is no Hell. For example, the spirit "Emmanuel" who possesses Pat Rodegast states: "Death is perfectly safe."[41] The spirits also teach that all men will reincarnate until they achieve perfection. In brief, the spirits agree on the nature and destiny of man.

There is also agreement on the importance of occult practices and the necessity of widespread contact with them. Also, the spirits are in total agreement that Jesus Christ is not the Savior of the world. (The Bible teaches He is.) Most interestingly, the spirits are in agreement that the idea of the devil and demons are merely human inventions. (The Bible teaches the devil and demons are real.)

13. Why do many channelers say their spirit guides are part of their unconscious mind?

Many channelers claim their spirit guides are a part of their "creative unconscious." They say this because they are uncomfortable with the idea that real spirits are actually possessing them. Channelers find it easier to believe the spirits are merely part of the newfound powers of their own mind or human genius. To deceive men, the spirits often go along with such labels.

Interestingly enough, modern parapsychology (the scientific study of the occult) has provided much support to relabel the activity of these spirits. Again, the spirits who desire to possess men find the relabeling of their activity to be good. Men who would never permit themselves to be possessed by spirits, might welcome the "scientific"-sounding idea that they are really contacting their own alleged "higher consciousness" or "divine mind." Once the spirits' activity is masked under the disguise of psychic powers, or the powers of the unconscious mind, their activity becomes unrecognizable for what it really is: true spirit contact. What is frightening here is that both the scientific community and psychics are redefining something supernatural and alien as really being something natural and human.[42]

In his classic book *The Screwtape Letters* Oxford scholar C. S. Lewis astutely portrays two devils talking to one another and planning their strategy:

> "Our policy, for the moment, is to conceal ourselves. Of course this has not always been so. We are really faced with a cruel dilemma. When the humans disbelieve in our existence we lose all the pleasing results of direct terrorism, and we make no magicians. On the other hand, when they believe in us, we cannot make them materialists and skeptics. At least, not yet. I have great hopes that we shall learn in due time how to emotionalize and mythologize their science to such an extent that what is, in effect, a belief in us (though not under that name) will creep in while the human mind remains closed to belief in the Enemy. The 'Life Force,' the worship of sex and some aspect of Psychoanalysis may here prove useful. If once we can produce our perfect work—the Materialist Magician, the man, not using, but veritably worshipping, what he vaguely calls 'Forces' while denying the existence of 'spirits'—then the end of the war will be in sight."[43]

Today even psychology is using its influence to promote the activity of spirits in a non-threatening psychological language. For example, we now have past-life therapy, inner-counselor therapy, transpersonal psychology, transcultural psychiatry, metapsychiatry, and shamanistic counseling, all of which involves or may verge on spiritism. Again, it is clear that certain concepts in modern psychology are becoming a major tool for camouflaging the demonic and expanding its influence in society under another name. Proof of this is that virtually every occult power or spirit manifestation has been "explained" psychologically or parapsychologically, or endorsed humanistically as the "new powers of the mind." And once psychology redefines these spirits as the hidden potential of the human mind, the goal of therapy will be to successfully tap into these new powers.[44] This approach agrees with the stated purposes of many of the spirits themselves who say their goal is to "empower" people to get in touch with their own "intuition," "higher Self," "creative sub-personality," or "divine potential," so that in the future *everyone* will become a channel for something.[45] In essence, the spirits desire man to view their activity as nothing more than the normal workings of the human mind. What they desire is invisibility.

Section III

The Theology of Channeling

14. What are the religious views of the spirits?

First, we will present a brief summary in which we compare the spirits' views with Bible teaching. Then we will quote the spirits themselves from channeled literature to document their teachings.

God

The spirits teach that God is an impersonal Force (an "It"), like electricity. It (God) has power but it cannot love. The Bible teaches that God is a personal, holy and loving God (John 3:16).

Jesus

The spirits teach that Jesus is an ascended master or a man just like us. The spirits say that Jesus has died and has now evolved to a higher state of existence just like others. The Bible teaches that Jesus is fully Man and fully God in one person. He is the only unique Son of God (John 1:1; Philippians 2:1-9; Titus 2:13).

Man

The spirits teach that man in his true nature is perfect and one essence with God. The Bible teaches that man is a created being who sinned by disobeying God, resulting in his being separated from God's fellowship (Genesis 1:27; 3:3-8).

Sin

The spirits teach that sin is merely ignorance of one's own deity. The Bible teaches that sin is disobedience of God's law (I John 3:4; 5:17).

Salvation

The spirits teach that salvation involves realizing that one is already God. Each man must accomplish this for himself by practicing various occult techniques. The Bible teaches that salvation involves receiving the gift of forgiveness of sins from God. Salvation has been provided for man by God's grace and is received by man through faith in Christ's death for us (Ephesians 1:7; 2:8, 9).

Death

The spirits teach that at death there is no judgment. It is merely a transition into the spirit world. The Bible teaches death brings judgment and entrance either into an eternal Heaven or Hell (Matthew 25:46; Hebrews 9:27).

Satan

The spirits teach there is no devil. The Bible teaches that Satan and his demons are real (Matthew 4:1-10; 8:16; 17:18).

Now we will cite the words of the spirits themselves concerning their religious teachings. As you read them carefully, ask yourself some questions. Are these teachings good or evil? Are they true or false? Are they what we would expect from deceitful demons or truly good spirits?

Teachings of the Spirits[46]

1. "Ramtha"—The spirit speaking through medium J. Z. Knight in Ramtha, *Voyage to the New World*, Ballentine, 1987; citations are listed by pages.

> **"Ramtha's" teaching on God:** Ramtha teaches the Christian God is an "idiotic deity." (p. 219); "... God, the principal, is all things..." (p. 250).

> **"Ramtha's" teaching on man:** "You are *God*." (p. 61); "God the Father is you." (p. 136); "Everyone is what you call a psychic..." (p. 139); "Love yourself... live in the moment, to exalt all that you are." (p. 149).

> **"Ramtha's" teaching on sin:** "... There is no such thing as evil." (p. 60); "...For 2,000 years we have been called sinful creatures ... [but] we are equal with God or Christ." (pp. 180-181).

> **"Ramtha's" teaching on salvation:** "Do not preach to this world—... the world doesn't need saving—leave it alone." (p. 130); "Relinquish guilt... do not live by rules, live by feelings.... You are the Lord of Hosts, *you* are

the Prince of Peace." (p. 149);; "Now to become enlightened is to make the priority of enlightenment first—the priority of love of Self *first*." (p. 227).

"Ramtha's" teaching on death: "God has never judged you or anyone." (p. 62); "No, there is no Hell and there is no devil." (p. 252).

"Ramtha's" teaching on Satan and demons: "Devil? I looked far and wide for the creature...I found him nowhere [but] I found him thriving in the hearts of frenzied entities in a fervor of madness to save the world from its sins...That is where he is. [Do] you understand?" (p. 252-253). "...The devil is not really evil...because he's really God...who else would he be?" (p. 251).

2. **"Jesus"**—The spirit who worked through medium Helen Schucman in *A Course in Miracles*, 1977; citations are listed by volume and page.

"Jesus' " teaching on God: "The recognition of God is the recognition of yourself. There is no separation of God and His creation." (1:136).

"Jesus' " teaching on Jesus: "There is nothing about me [Jesus] that you cannot attain." (1:5); "Christ waits for your acceptance of Him as yourself." (1:187); "Is [Jesus] the Christ? O yes, along with you." (1:83).

"Jesus' " teaching on man: "God's Name is holy, but no holier than yours. To call upon His Name is but to call upon your own." (2:334); "You are the Holy Son of God Himself." (2:353-54).

"Jesus' " teaching on sin: "...Sin does not exist." (3:81); "Sin is the grand illusion...joyously [release] one another from the belief in sin." (1:375, 377-78); "See no one, then, as guilty ...[within all men] there is perfect innocence."; "No one is punished for sins [and you] are not sinners." (1:88).

"Jesus' " teaching on salvation: "[Divine] Forgiveness, then, is an illusion..." (3:79); "[It is] a terrible misperception that God Himself [judged] His own Son on behalf of salvation ....It is so essential that all such thinking be dispelled that we must be sure that nothing of this kind remains in your mind. I was not 'punished' because you were bad." (1:32-33, 87); "A sense of separation from God is the only lack you really need to correct."; "Salvation is nothing more than 'right-mindedness'..."; "...you are one with God." (1:11,53; 2:125); "Do not make the pathetic error of 'clinging to the old rugged cross'.... This is not the gospel I.... intended to offer you." (1:47).

"Jesus' " teaching on death: "There is no death, but there is a belief in death." (1:46); "Death is the central dream from which all illusions stem." (3:63).

3. "Seth"—The spirit speaking through Jane Roberts and written down by her husband in *Seth Speaks*, Prentice Hall, 1972; citations are listed by pages.

"Seth's" teaching on God: God is "All That Is." (p. 405).

"Seth's" teaching on Jesus: "He [Jesus] will not come to reward the righteous and send evildoers to eternal doom." (p. 389).

"Seth's" teaching on sin: "A strong belief in such [concepts of good and evil] is highly detrimental..." (p. 191).

"Seth's" teaching on salvation: "...The soul...is not something you must save or redeem, and it is also something you cannot lose." (p. 89).

"Seth's" teaching on Satan and demons: "...The devil is a projection of your own psyche ...." (p. 7); "...There are no devils or demons ..." (p. 405).

4. "Lilly" and other spirits channeled through medium Ruth Montgomery. (Note: Some of the following statements are Montgomery's although they reflect the teachings of the spirits which she has adopted as her own belief.)

The spirits' teaching on God: "God is the name of What Is." (R.M., *Here and Hereafter*, Fawcett Crest, 1968, p. 74).

The spirits' teaching on man: "...God wishes that it [psychic ability] be utilized and developed to the fullest potential." (R.M., *A Search for Truth,* Bantam, 1968, p. 160); " . . . We are God . . ." (R.M., *A World Beyond*, Fawcett Crest, 1972, p. 12).

The spirits' teaching on death: "There is no such thing as death." (Ibid., p. 66); "God punishes no man." (R.M., *Here and Hereafter,* Fawcett Crest, 1968, p. 174).

The spirits' teaching on Satan and demons: "I have seen no signs of a devil on this side of the veil ['veil' here means death]." (R.M., *A World Beyond*, Fawcett Crest, 1972, p. 64); "The devil was not a person ever . . ." (Ibid., p. 65).

5. Various spirits who allegedly knew Jesus on earth written through medium Kahlil Gibran in *Jesus, the Son of Man* (New York, A. A. Knopf, 1959); citations are listed by pages.

The spirits' views on God: "Israel should have another God . . ." (p. 32).

The spirits' views on Jesus: "Jesus the Nazarene was born and reared like ourselves . . . He was [only] a man."; "Jesus was a man and not a god . . . It's a pity his followers seek to make a god of such a sage." (Ibid., pp. 43, 109, 113).

Now consider the content of what you have just read. Do these spirits deny there is a devil when Jesus taught that Satan was a real, personal being (Matthew 4:1-10)? Do the spirits endorse the occult when God forbids it? (Deuteronomy 18:9-12). Why do you think the spirits claim men are not sinners when all men know in their hearts they are? Why do the spirits teach that God is impersonal when God has revealed Himself in the Bible as a personal Being? Why do the spirits teach man to be selfish when such behavior is universally condemned? Why do the spirits deny that Christ died to forgive men's sins when Christ Himself taught this was the very reason He came? (Matthew 20:28). Why do the spirits claim Jesus was simply a man when all the evidence proves He was God-Incarnate, the only begotten Son of God? He Himself taught this (John 3:16; 5:18; 10:30; 14:6). Why do the spirits say men are God, when we know *we* are not God? Why do the spirits deny the existence of evil when its reality is obvious to all? The point is this. The religious teachings of the spirits are exactly what one might expect from demons. The irony is that the very theory that is most probably true, that Satan and demons do exist, is the one most rarely considered.

15. What does the Bible say about channeling?

The first historical incidence of channeling is recorded in the Bible in Genesis Chapter 3. There in the Garden of Eden the devil used the serpent as a "channel" to trick Eve (Genesis 3:1-5; II Corinthians 11:3; Revelation 12:9). Through channeling, the devil deceived man into doubting God, with serious consequences. Significantly, there are compelling reasons for believing that the basic reality of channeling that is suggested here has never altered, either as to its (1) origin (the devil or demons); (2) result (spiritual deception which undermines trust in God) (3) consequences (divine judgment; Genesis 3:13-19; Deuteronomy 18:9-13). Channeling is thus condemned in the Bible as an evil practice before God. It is rejected because it is a form of spiritism which involves contact with demons and the spreading of their false teachings.

The Bible further teaches that "in later times some will fall away from the faith, paying attention to deceitful spirits and doctrines of demons" (I Timothy 4:1). Spiritistic teachings pervert the nature of God, lie about Christ and distort the way of salvation. Those who trust spiritistic teachings face judgment at death. On the authority of one no less than Christ Himself we discover that Hell is a real place (Matthew 25:46; Luke 16:19-31). The demons who assure men that sin is not real and Hell does not exist are bringing eternal ruin to those who trust them.

The Bible instructs man to reject every form of spiritism as something evil and an encounter with lying spirits. Channeling is a form of spiritual warfare with the souls of men at stake (II Corinthians 4:4). This is why both channeling itself and following the teaching of the channelers are condemned in Scripture as rebellion against God and as courting His judgment. An example of this is King Manasseh of Judah in ancient Israel. "He practiced witchcraft, used divination, practiced sorcery and dealt with mediums and spiritists. He did much evil in the sight of the Lord, provoking Him to anger" (II Chronicles 33:2-6). Likewise in Deuteronomy 18:9-12 God warns His people that "There shall not be found among you anyone...who uses divination, who practices witchcraft, who is a spiritist, or who calls up the dead. For whoever does these things is detestable to the Lord...." The phrase "who is a spiritist" clearly condemns all aspects of channeling.

Section IV

Channeling
and Related Issues

16. Is there any relationship between hypnosis, multiple personality and channeling?

First, hypnosis is an altered state of consciousness that may open people to the entrance of spirits. In fact, many mediums first trained for spirit contact through the practice of hypnosis.[47] Historically, hypnosis has had a long history of occult associations, from yoga to mesmerism. To us, hypnosis' therapeutic value is debatable (not because it is never helpful but because of other concerns for which there are still no answers). And quite clearly, there is an obvious occult use of hypnosis so that caution is urged.[48] For example, as already stated, many mediums admit their first spirit contact took place under hypnosis. Others have used hypnosis as a means of developing psychic powers. The simple truth is that the state of hypnosis is an especially useful state of mind for anyone who has wanted to learn channeling.[49]

The relationship between multiple personality and channeling presents a dilemma because these conditions can be difficult to distinguish.

Here is an example of the relationship that may exist between channeling and multiple personality. One or two additional personalities (called multiple personality) may be explained as a consequence of the natural breakdown of the human mind. However, the cases of dozens or scores of personalities as the 92 personalities cited in the book *When Rabbit Howls* (written by the "entities" themselves) are often close enough to classical spiritism that possession by truly supernatural beings appears to explain these cases more adequately.[50] In fact, there are even a number of secular researchers of multiple personalities who admit that in many cases they are dealing with spirit-possession and not true multiple personality.[51] What is disturbing is that multiple personalities that appear to result from simple spirit-possession are being treated as a fascinating new area of human potential and scientific exploration. The medical goal today is to "integrate" the multiple personalities back into one original personality. Doctors seek to help patients accept their different personalities and permit them to continue to inhabit their body—perhaps under the leadership of the "dominant" personality. If these multiple personalities are really different spirits, then professional psychologists, who believe they are helping people, are really helping them to accept their own demonization. Some psychologists even refer to the multiple personalities as separate beings, literally as "entities," because this is exactly how these personalities act.[52] A biblical example of "multiple personality" that was certainly demonic was the Gerasenes' demoniac in Luke 8:28,30.

17. What else is channeling related to?

The practice of spiritism does not arrive in a clearly marked package today. Often one needs to look beneath the surface of a given practice or phenomenon to uncover the spiritistic roots or source of power. Examples of this are most near-death experiences[53], water and other dowsing[54], UFO's[55], aspects of parapsychology[56], some forms of mysticism[57], and many forms of "spiritual" healing and holistic health practices.[58]

Channeling sometimes bears a relationship to mental illness. One discovers many mental patients who are mentally ill precisely because they are demonized.[59] This is born out by the research of German psychiatrist and parapsychologist Hans Bender who coined the term "mediumistic psychosis"[60]; by theologian and psychologist Kurt Koch[61]; and by clinical psychologist and Swedenborgian Wilson Van Dusen, who has examined thousands of patients and noted the parallels to spiritistic experiences and phenomena.[62]

18. Are cults related to channeling?

There is a direct relationship between the origin of hundreds of cults and the phenomenon of channeling. Channeling is how they began, and the reason for this is a logical one. To illustrate, after Japan was dramatically defeated in World War II, the people's faith in the divine status of the Japanese emperor was shattered. A spiritual vacuum arose that was filled by scores of new cults, many of which began powerfully through spirit contact and channeled messages.[63] One such example of this was the Odoru Shukyo sect begun by Kitamura Sayo in 1945. Sayo claimed, characteristically, that a Shinto deity "took possession of her" to give divine revelations.[63a]

In the U.S. we have experienced a similar situation. This has occurred through the impact of secularism and other humanist beliefs which for millions has resulted in the loss of faith in God. This resulted in a spiritual vacuum—and vacuums are always filled by something.

In this case the vacuum was filled by hundreds of American cults and sects that are related to or involved with channeling.[64] In America some educators go so far as to assert that channeling "appears to be an essential element in the origins of virtually all of the great spiritual paths."[65]

But why should this be true? The reason is simple. Channeling and religion go hand-in-hand because the purpose of the spirits is to provide men with a religious belief that insulates against belief in Christ.

The Bible teaches, "The whole world lies in the power of the evil one" and that Satan "blinds the minds" of unbelievers (II Corinthians 4:4; I John 5:19).

A quick examination of religions in our world today that are associated with channeling include Islamism, Hinduism, Buddhism, Shintoism and Animism.[66] In addition, some sects or cults have developed in America at least in part as a result of channeling. Among the gurus are Paramahansa Yogananda (Self-Realization Fellowship), Krishnamurti, Rajneesh, Sri Chinmoy, and Ram Dass, to name just a few.[67]

Other new religions and cults in America that are related to channeling are Alice Bailey's Lucius Trust, Paul Twitchell's Eckankar, David Berg's The Children of God (the Love Family), Sun Myung Moon's Unification Church, Rudolph Steiner's Anthroposophy, Earlyne Chaney's Astara, Elizabeth Claire Prophet's Church Universal and Triumphant, Guy Ballard's The Mighty I Am, Joseph Smith's Mormonism (the angel "Moroni"), Mary Baker Eddy's Christian Science—again, just to name a few.[68] When one stops to think about it, isn't it amazing that all of these religions have been touched by channeling? It is sobering indeed to realize that all of these religions have been influenced by channeling when the God of the Bible absolutely forbids it.

(2) The testimony of occultists themselves, whether magicians, psychics, channelers, mediums or Satanists indicate they are very much aware of the reality of spiritual evil, however they may choose to define it. Many of them believe in literal evil spirits and have had personal encounters with them. Such encounters leave little doubt as to their malevolent nature.[85]

(3) Another line of evidence involves the experience of demon-possession, which occurs in nearly every culture and religion, ancient or modern.[86] Former witch Doreen Irvine declares, "Demon-possession is real, very real, and is increasing at an alarming rate in this present day and age."[87] Naturally, the very act of a spirit invading and controlling a person implies, even demands, hostility and malice. And it is usually the occultist who gets possessed. In his text *People of the Lie,* psychiatrist M. Scott Peck, author of the best-selling *The Road Less Traveled* observes, "It seems clear from the literature on possession that a majority of cases have had involvement with the occult—a frequency far greater than might be expected in the general population."[88] (See Question 5.)

(4) A fourth reason suggesting the reality of a real devil is the Bible. Because the Bible is the Word of God, what it says about the existence of a personal devil is obviously true; therefore in light of the abundance of data supporting its claim to divine inspiration, we may assume its statements about Satan are reliable. If one believes in the truth of the Bible, then it is impossible to doubt the reality of the devil. Jesus Christ Himself believed in the reality of Satan and demons. And no one else could speak with more authority. No one else in history directly claimed to be God (John 5:18; 10:30; 14:9) and proved the truth of His claim by literally rising from the dead (Matthew 20:18,19; Luke 1:1-4 with John 20:24-28; Acts 1:3).[88a]

(5) Finally, the teachings of the spirits universally oppose the Bible. The most logical explanation for their single-mindedness is that they are the very spirits that the Bible exposes as demons.

In addition some of the most brilliant minds of our modern era have accepted the reality of demons. The brilliant Christian apologist C. S. Lewis said in regard to their existence, "It seems to me to explain a good many facts. It agrees with the plain sense of Scripture, the tradition of Christendom, and the beliefs of most men at most times. And it conflicts with nothing that any of the sciences has shown to be true."[88b] Lawyer and theologian Dr. John Warwick Montgomery asserts, "The problem involved in determining whether demon-possession occurs and whether witchcraft works is absurdly simple. The documentation is overwhelming."[89] He also states, "There is overwhelming extra-biblical data and empirical confirmation of the scriptural claims" regarding the existence of a personal devil and demons.[90]

In brief, when one considers not only the divine authority of the Bible and the testimony of Christ who, as God, was also an infallible authority, but also the consensus of history and religion, the testimony of active occultists, the phenomenon of possession, and the hostility to biblical revelation displayed in spiritistic literature, one is hard-pressed to maintain simply that demons do not exist. In the end, one either trusts the spirits and ignores the facts or one trusts the facts and ignores the spirits.

23. Do demons have a plan for men's lives?

The principal goal of a demon is spiritual deception which is camouflaged or invisible. They are masters of impersonating those who have died. The Bible tells us demons are personal evil beings from another dimension who would seek to camouflage themselves for hidden purposes. The disguises range from promoting themselves as myth to the opposite extreme of promoting themselves as the ultimate reality, or God Himself. And, indeed, the majority of people in our culture either believe that Satan does not exist or that psychic powers, contacts with spirits and channeling spirits are actually divine practices and represent contact with God.

In the world today most men recognize the existence of evil, but few men recognize the existence of the devil who accounts for much of that evil. The devil can get us thinking about our own self-interests so that we are not concerned with the state of our soul. The end result is that this is the greatest threat any man can face (Matthew 16:26; Luke 12:20). In brief, we see that in the world today we may believe in a thousand little evils, but we do not believe in the one Evil (Satan) that is responsible for many of them. Our greatest danger is when we do not recognize a Threat that outweighs every other threat.

The Bible warns us of the devil's techniques and goes all the way back to "Day One" (II Corinthians 2:11; 11:3; Ephesians 6:11). The Bible reports the devil lied to man in the Garden in two ways. First, he told man, "You shall be as God." Second, he promised, "You shall not die." Isn't it interesting that his spirits have not deviated from their master's first lies? If channeled beings are not demons, then the consistency and persistence of these themes throughout the history of spiritistic revelations is nothing short of amazing. Not only is this amazing—but why would channeled spirits who have always been hostile to the Bible still use the very lies the Bible reports Satan used back in the Garden?

What can you say to the unbeliever who does not accept the Bible as authoritative in his life and who views the story of Adam, Eve, and Satan in the Garden as just another myth? Consider the following:

1. Why is it that channeled spirits who are usually considered to be "good" beings model their teachings on what so many modern men believe is a false myth?

2. Why would good spirits want to identify themselves in any way with the most terrible and despicable spirit-being in the Bible?

3. Could it be the reason these spirits have not changed their message is because that is their message, has always been their message, and because what the Bible says is true?

4. Further, to the person who does not believe the Bible, how could the Bible accurately describe what these spirits say?

5. Finally, why is it that many former occultists who have been deeply involved with the spirits have said that the only way to escape from those spirits is through the Christ of the Bible?

24. What evidence would lead a thinking person to conclude that the actions of the channeled spirits suggest their nature is evil?

The entire history of the influence of these beings upon humanity suggests their nature is evil. That these spirits are evil can be documented from history, religion, psychology, and especially from the experiences of channelers themselves as we will see in our next two questions. Because channeling is contact with demons, it is an evil practice by itself, and it is also one that leads to countless other evils. Among these are immorality, crime, fraud and physical and spiritual destruction. We saw earlier that the spirits whose teachings reject God and lie about Christ cannot be considered good.

Professor Edmund Gruss mentions several cases of murder committed on the advice of the spirits. In one case a 15-year-old daughter murdered her father. In another case a 77-year-old man was literally forced to kill his wife in self-defense because she believed the lies the spirits told her about his unfaithfulness.[91] There are many such cases. One of us (Weldon) talked with a serial killer whose "religious commission" was to travel the countryside murdering people his spirit guide told him "deserved to die." (The spirits always provided a way for him to dispose of the body safely so they could not be discovered.) Historically the spirits have caused the murder of hundreds of thousands of children and adults through human sacrifice[92] (including probably the recent Atlanta child murders[92]); they have helped start revolutions (including the Mexican Revolution of 1910[93]) and their teachings have sapped the moral strength of countless numbers. They have done this by leading men to commit other evil acts which they otherwise would not have committed.

Jesus Himself called the devil "a liar and a murderer" from the beginning (John 8:44). Those who play into his hands can expect great promises and excitement to begin with, but little else than deceit and destruction in the long run.

On a more practical level, if the channeled revelations suggesting "there is no death" become widely accepted, then people may become more open to death itself. In addition there are spiritistically-engineered revelations from thousands of "near-death" experiences extolling the glories of death and the afterlife. People have a heart attack or are in a near-fatal car crash and have an out-of-the-body experience where they encounter a "being of light," the dead, and feelings of great peace and love. Almost all of them say they regret being "brought back" and they look forward to death with great expectation.

The combination of channeled revelations about death and the near-death experiences may lead to an increase in suicide or euthanasia. Consider one incident. San Francisco is a city known for both its romance and its perversions. In San Francisco, "the man and woman kissed each other time after time, then turned their backs to the bay and, holding hands, tumbled backward off the Golden Gate Bridge to their deaths." The man left a suicide note in his car that indicated he had been "called" to enter the "other world." The note ended: "I love you all; wish I could stay, but I must hurry. The suspense is killing me."[94] The suspense killed him all right.

Channeling teaches this life is not the end (annihilation) and that there is no judgment. If this life is simply too difficult or unpleasant, why *not* take the easy way out? Why not enter a world you have been promised is far more glorious? Death, after all, is claimed to be a friend. In fact, the spirits often encourage this. We have read innumerable cases where the "loving" spirits have deliberately induced emotional dependence upon their advice and then at a moment of weakness encouraged their contact to commit suicide.[95] And this has been occurring for decades, probably even centuries. In the 1920 text *The Menace of Spiritualism*, case after case of tragedy is listed. The foreword by Bernard Vaughan, S.J., states,

> "This very morning I heard of a girl, who being told in a seance by her deceased lover that he would not live on the other side without her, drowned herself to join him, not, I fancy, in heaven...."[96]

25. Do channelers ever suspect the spirits may not be who they claim?

Many channelers seem to have periods of genuine doubt as to the nature of these beings. A more objective assessment might indicate they are merely manipulated to perform the occult work of otherworldly entities of dubious character and highly questionable intent. Too often the spiritist's faith is one whose entire basis is founded upon a naive trust undergirded through a romance of emotion and experience.

Nevertheless the channelers do have their doubts. These doubts are carefully handled by the entities themselves. For example, one of Elisabeth Kubler-Ross' spirit guides, "Salem," "proved" he wasn't a demon to a skeptical priest by allowing himself to be soaked with "holy water"—while in fully-materialized form. He was supposed to disappear but didn't, thus "proving" he was not a demon.[97]

Mohammad was not certain if he was possessed by a jinn (an Islamic demon) in receiving the revelations of the Koran, but was persuaded otherwise.[98]

When unbiblical revelations started coming from Edgar Cayce's unconscious trance sessions, the famous seer openly wondered if, "The devil might be tempting me to do his work by operating through me when I was conceited enough to think God had given me special power." After his first unbiblical reading on reincarnation he replied, "If ever the devil was going to play a trick on me, this would be it."[99] J. Z. Knight who channels "Ramtha" went through a period where she felt he might be a demon but was eventually persuaded to trust him.[100]

Another example is Uri Geller, famous for bending spoons and knives by psychic power. Both Geller and his teacher, parapsychologist Andrija Puharich, M.D., had an uneasy feeling that there was something "funny" or "wrong" about their spirit contacts. They suspected they were being "played with" and wondered if the entities themselves were unstable.[101] There are many other cases where channels have been uneasy or apprehensive over the exact nature of their encounters.

26. Are there actual cases where channeling has become destructive?

As an introduction, consider the case of Bill Slater, head of BBC television drama. One evening, after attending "an impromptu seance" with a Ouija board, he went home. In the early hours of the morning:

> "I found myself half-awake, knowing there was some kind of presence massing itself on my chest; it was, to my certain knowledge, making every effort to take over my mind and body. It cost me considerable will-power to concentrate all my faculties to push the thing away, and for what seemed like twenty minutes this spiritual tussle went on between this awful presence and myself. Needless to say, although before going to bed I had felt perfectly happy and at ease with a very good friend, in a flat I knew well, I was now absolutely terrified—I have never known such fear since. I was finally able to call my friend's name; he woke up, put on the light, and was astonished to find me well-nigh a gibbering idiot. I have never since had any psychic experience."[102]

Besides the above flirt with the demonic, there are many cases where occultic activity has directly resulted in the destruction of human life. It is not just that there are a few cases, the fact is there are thousands of them littered throughout the history of religion, occultism, spiritism, and parapsychology—mental illness, suicide, physical crippling, blindness,[103] death. People who would never think of playing Russian Roulette with a gun, even once, or who would never deliberately take a dangerous drug, have a very good reason for their decisions. The odds of disaster are too high. Yet the odds of harming oneself from occultic practices are apparently just as high or higher.[104] What is amazing is that the evidence is there for all to see and yet it is ignored.

In the Bible, demons are presented as inflicting numerous physical and psychological ailments upon their victims.

Many of these parallel today's cases of channeling. While it must be stressed that most illness is not demonically wrought, the array of symptoms suggest the possibility of a virtual monopoly over the workings of the human mind and body: skin disease (Job 2:7), destructive and irrational acts (Matthew 8:28; Luke 8:27), deafness and inability to speak (Mark 9:25; Luke 11:14), epileptic-like seizures (Matthew 17:15; Mark 9:17; Luke 9:39), blindness (Matthew 12:22), tormenting pain (Revelation 9:1-11), insanity (Luke 8:26-35), severe physical deformity (Luke 13:11-17), and other symptoms. Demons can give a person supernatural strength (Luke 8:29) or attempt to murder them (Matthew 17:15,18).

Not unexpectedly, there are numerous accounts of mediums, channelers and occultists or those who frequent them suffering physically in a variety of ways from their practice (ill health, alcoholism, spirit attacks, early deaths, etc.).

Most people do not know the famous medium Arthur Ford became a morphine addict and alcoholic, which caused him no end of grief much of his life.[105] Bishop Pike died a tragic death from his involvement in spiritism.[106] Medium Jane Roberts died at the young age of 47. Others became addicted to drugs.[107] Medium Edgar Cayce, a large man of 6′ 2″, died in misery weighing a mere 60 pounds, apparently physiologically "burned out" from giving too many psychic readings. The biography on Cayce by Joseph Millard reveals the extent of suffering Cayce's occultic involvement cost him—from psychic attacks to mysterious fires, the periodic loss of his voice, erratic personality changes and emotional torments, constant "bad luck" and personal setback, and guilt induced by psychic readings that ruined others' lives.[108] Many channelers seem to succumb to various vices later in life, from sexual immorality[109] to numbing their conscience[110], to alcoholism and drug addiction[111], to crime and worse.[112]

M. Lamar Keene spent 13 years among professional mediums as a famous (although fraudulent) medium. In his public confession, *The Psychic Mafia*, he observes,

> "All the mediums I've known or known about have had tragic endings. The Fox sisters, who started it all, wound up as alcoholic derelicts. William Slade, famed for his slate-writing tricks, died insane in a Michigan sanitarium. Margery, the medium, lay on her deathbed a hopeless drunk. The celebrated Arthur Ford fought the battle of the bottle till the very end and lost.... Wherever I looked it was the same: mediums, at

the end of a tawdry life, dying a tawdry death.
... I was sick and tired of the whole business—
the fraud bit, the drug bit, the drinking bit, the
entire thing...."[113]

Spiritist and guru Sri Chinmoy, a spiritual advisor at the United Nations observes, "Many, many black magicians and people who deal with spirits have been strangled or killed. I know because I've been near quite a few of these cases."[114]

Dr. Kurt Koch observed after 45 years of counseling the occultly oppressed that from his own experience "numerous cases of suicides, fatal accidents, strokes and insanity are to be observed among occult practitioners." And that "anyone who has had to observe for 45 years the effects of spiritism can only warn people with all the strength at his disposal."[115]

In addition, over many years, the very act of channeling itself appears to have a destructive effect upon the human body. It is as if there is a type of, for lack of a better word, "psychic vampirism" at work which slowly eats away at a person's physical constitution.[116] Time and again in the lives of psychics, mediums and spiritists, we have observed the power of the spirits in holding their captives to do their will (II Timothy 2:24-26). When one attempts to suppress their channeling or mediumship, for example, the result will frequently be symptoms of disease or other serious problems, forcing a return to the practice.[117] What is doubly tragic is that for all these people it started out so good, so promising. Consider the case of "Carl" as a final illustration.

Carl was a qualified psychologist with a degree in physics and a personal interest in religion (especially Christianity) and parapsychology, or the scientific study of the occult. In fact, he became a leading parapsychologist. His personal psychic abilities amazed not only himself but those who knew him. He was enormously excited by Aldous Huxley's *Doors of Perception*; what Huxley achieved by drugs Carl was certain he could achieve by psychic means: that, and perhaps more. Although fascinated by Christianity, Carl was convinced that the modern churches were corrupting the original teachings of Christ. Hence he sought "true Christianity" through occult means.

Consumed with a desire to find "original Christianity," he became personally involved in reincarnation research and astral travel. As his studies and involvement in the psychic world continued, he explored realm after realm. He was bright and enthusiastic, not to mention careful. Most of all he was *certain* he was on the road to vast personal discoveries. He had, in his view, all the right motives—and talent, abilities and opportunities to complement them.

Eventually a mid-Western university offered Carl a professorship and allowed him to both teach and continue his experiments, which provided numerous psychic and mystical experiences. Gradually, however, Carl admitted to himself that some deep alteration was taking place inside of him.[118] He had earlier encountered some gnawing doubts about the fundamental nature of his spiritual path but he suppressed them because they were too uncomfortable in their implications. Any doubt as to what kind of spirit was leading him could mean a total revision of his work; it could even mean resigning his professorship and renouncing his parapsychological research.[119]

Giving up his research would have been costly, but after years of painstaking effort, benevolent motives and great enthusiasm, Carl became consumed by forces so evil he ended up as an incoherent vegetable requiring exorcism and 11 months of hospitalization.

His eventual renouncement of all study and research in parapsychology was deplored by fellow colleagues who never learned the real reason for his strange disappearance from the community. He finally had to conclude,

> "Solemnly and of my own free will I wish to acknowledge that knowingly and freely I entered into possession by an evil spirit. And, although that spirit came to me under the guise of saving me, perfecting me, helping me to help others, I knew all along it was evil."[120]

27. What logical evidence would lead channelers to acknowledge their own peril, and what can channelers do to escape the consequences that must befall them?

We believe we have already presented sufficient evidence to show that these spirits are demons and that, as such, the life of the channeler is at risk. Certainly his spiritual life is at risk. Those who have been involved in channeling need to acknowledge their peril—as well as their responsibility to others they may think they are helping.

The Bible commands and warns us to "test the spirits" (I John 4:1). If the spirits' teachings do not agree with the words of God, then no matter what one thinks or feels, they cannot be from God. If they claim this then they are lying.

There is only one path of safety for a channeler—repentance from sin and faith in Christ.

28. Have any channelers turned to God from channeling?

Victor Ernest, author of *I Talked with Spirits,* Ben Alexander, author of *Out From Darkness,* and Raphel Gasson, author of *The Challenging Counterfeit,* are three public examples of individuals who came to recognize that the spirits they thought were their guides and friends were, in fact, evil spirits bent on their destruction. They were delivered from their power, not without struggle, by the only effective method available—a complete renouncing of their practices before God and a turning to Christ as personal Lord and Savior.[121]

God teaches these practices will destroy you in the long run. They may seem helpful now, but appearances can be deceptive. There are many things in life which begin good and end tragically. Test the spirits to see if they are of God (I John 4:1). Read this booklet again; examine our arguments. If there is even a chance we are correct, then you owe it to yourself, to your family and children, to your friends and clients, to be certain the spirits are not deceiving you. The following prayer is suggested for those who have been involved in channeling.

> Dear God, these spirits are not of You and I ask for Your protection from them. I confess my sin of seeking what You have forbidden and I renounce these spirits and all involvement with them. I ask Jesus Christ to enter my life and to be my Lord and Savior. I recognize this is a solemn decision that You take very seriously. I believe that on the cross Jesus Christ died for my sin and I receive Him into my life now. My commitment to You is that I will follow Him and not the spirits. I ask for Your help in doing this. Amen.

If you prayed this prayer, there are several things you need to do to grow in the Christian life. Start to read a modern translation Bible and find a good church that honors Christ. Tell someone you have just become a Christian so they may pray for you and encourage you in your new life with Christ. (Sometimes, unfortunately Christians may not understand your experiences; persevere until you find a Christian friend who can pray with you and help you grow spiritually.) And remember, Jesus Himself said, "All authority has been given to Me in Heaven and on earth ... I am with you always, even to the end of the age" (Matthew 28:18-20).

Conclusion

For anyone who may be unnecessarily concerned over the influence of the demonic in his life we encourage you to remember that although spiritual warfare exists, the devil and his demons are subject to the authority of God and present no danger to the average Christian seeking to do God's will. (See Eph. 6:11-13; James 4:7; I John 4:4.) For the non-Christian (or Christian) involved in any form of the occult, there must be an immediate ceasing of all activity and a turning of one's life over to Christ as Lord. Dr. Kurt Koch's book *Occult Bondage and Deliverance* (Kregal, 1972) contains valuable insight for those seeking deliverance.

Recommended Reading

Ankerberg, John, and Weldon, John, *The Facts on The New Age Movement* (Chattanooga, TN: The John Ankerberg Evangelistic Association, 1988).

Gasson, Raphael, *The Challenging Counterfeit*, Logos [Bridge], 1970.

Earnest, Victor, *I Talked with Spirits*, Tyndale House, 1971.

North, Gary, *Unholy Spirits: Occultism and New Age Humanism*, Dominion Press, 1986.

Montgomery, John Warwick (ed.), *Demon Possession: A Medical, Historical, Anthropological and Theological Symposium*, Bethany Fellowship, 1976.

Unger, Merril, *The Haunting of Bishop Pike*, Tyndale House, 1971.

———, *Biblical Demonology: A Study of the Spiritual Forces Behind the Present World Unrest*, Scripture Press, 1971.

———, *Demons in the World Today*, Tyndale House, 1972.

Irvine, Doreen, *Freed from Witchcraft*, Thomas Nelson, 1973.

Gruss, Edmond, *The Ouija Board: Doorway to the Occult*, Moody, 1975.

Keene, M. Lamar, *The Psychic Mafia: The True and Shocking Confessions of a Famous Medium*, St. Martin's Press, 1976.

Koch, Kurt, and Lechler, Alfred, *Occult Bondage and Deliverance*, Kregel, 1970.

Michaelsen, Johanna, *The Beautiful Side of Evil*, Harvest House, 1982.

Weldon, John, and Levitt, Zola, *Psychic Healing: An Exposé of an Occult Phenomenon*, Moody Press, 1982.

Nevius, John L., *Demon Possession*, Kregel, 1970, rpt.

Spiritual Counterfeits Project, *Eckankar: A Hard Look at a New Religion*, SCP Journal, Berkeley, CA, 1979.

Spiritual Counterfeits Project, *Spiritism: The Medium and the Message*, SCP Journal, Berkeley, CA, 1987.

Miller, Elliott, "Channeling: Spiritistic Revelation for the New Age," *Christian Research Journal*, Fall, 1987.

Goodrick-Clarke, Nicholas, *The Occult Roots of Naziism: the Ariosophists of Austria and Germany 1890-1935*, The Aquarian Press [England], 1985.

Angebert, Jean-Michel, *The Occult and the Third Reich*, McGraw-Hill, 1975.

Alexander, Ben, *Out From Darkness: The True Story of a Medium Who Escapes the Occult*, College Press, 1986.

Footnotes

1. Alan Gauld, *The Founders of Psychical Research* (New York: Schocken Books, 1968), p. 24.

2. William James, "Report on Mrs. Piper's Hodgson Control," *Proceedings of the English Society for Psychical Research*, Vol. 23, pp. 1-121, from Jon Klimo, *Channeling: Investigations on Receiving Information from Paranormal Sources* (Los Angeles: Jeremy P. Tarcher, Inc., 1987), p. 238.

3. Klimo, op. cit., pp. 1, 24,27; Brooks Alexander, "Theology From the Twilight Zone," *Christianity Today*, September 18, 1987, p. 22.

4. Nina Easton, "Shirley MacLaine's Mysticism for the Masses," *The Los Angeles Times Magazine*, September 6, 1987, p. 33; Klimo, op. cit., pp. 44, 48-49; Katherine Lowry, "Channelers: Mouthpieces of the Spirits," *Omni* Magazine, October 1987, p. 22.

5. Slater Brown, *The Heyday of Spiritualism* (New York: Pocket Books, 1972), pp. 159-160.

6. Nandor Fodor cites the *North American Review*, April 1855, as accurate in giving the figure of nearly two million spiritists in 1855 (Nandor Fodor, *An Encyclopedia of Psychic Science* (Secaucus, NJ: Citadel, 1974), p. 362; Alfred Douglas, *Extra-Sensory Powers: A Century of Psychical Research* (Woodstock, New York: Overlook Press, 1977), p. 54. On the authority of the editor of the *Home Journal* he cites 40,000 spiritualists in New York in 1853; Gauld, op. cit., p. 15.

7. This is evident from any number of historical studies. See Paul Kurtz, "Introduction: More Than a Century of Psychical Research," in Paul Kurtz (ed.), *A Skeptic's Handbook of Parapsychology* (Buffalo, NY: Prometheus, 1985), pp. xii-xiv; John Beloff, "Historical Overview" in Benjamin B. Wolman (ed.), *Handbook of Parapsychology* (New York: Van Nostrand Reinhold, 1977), pp. 4-7; J. B. Rhine, "A Century of Parapsychology" in Martin Ebon (ed.), *The Signet Handbook of Parapsychology* (New York: Signet, 1978), p. 11.

8. See e.g., E. J. Dingwall, "The Need for Responsibility in Parapsychology: My Sixty Years in Psychical Research" in Paul Kurtz, op. cit., pp. 161, 174.

9. Lynn Smith, "The New Chic Metaphysical Fad of Channeling," *Los Angeles Times*, December 5, 1986, Part 5.

10. Easton, op. cit., pp. 8-10, 32-34; Klimo, op. cit., p. 49; John Ankerberg and John Weldon, *The Facts on The New Age Movement* (Chattanooga, TN: The John Ankerberg Evangelistic Association, 1988), pp. 6-7, 13-15.

11. Brooks Alexander, op. cit., p. 22; Klimo, op. cit., p. 42.

12. Klimo, op. cit., pp. 4-6, 62-68; Easton, op. cit., p. 10. Various magazines devoted exclusively to channeling include *Spirit Speaks, Metapsychology: The Journal of Discarnate Intelligence* and *The Channel Sourceletter* (Ottawa).

13. e.g., Mark Vaz, "Psychic!—The Many Faces of Kevin Ryerson" (Interview), *Yoga Journal*, July/August 1986, pp. 26-29, 92; Klimo, op. cit., pp. 3, 20, 39, 64-69, 131-132, 167, 237-253, 205-320; Stephan Schwartz, *The Secret Vaults of Time: Psychic Archaeology and the Quest for Man's Beginning* (New York: Grosset & Dunlap, 1978); Gerald G. Jampolsky, *Goodbye to Guilt: Releasing Fear Through Forgiveness* (New York: Bantam, 1985), (based on *A Course in Miracles*); Jane Roberts, *Adventures in Consciousness: An Introduction to Aspect Psychology* (1975); John Weldon and Zola Levitt, *Psychic Healing* (Chicago: Moody Press, 1982), pp. 7-22, 42-46.

13a. A. Harwood, *Rx: Spiritist as Needed* (New York: John Wiley & Sons, 1977), cited in Albert Villoldo and Stanley Krippner, *Healing States: A Journey Into the World of Spiritual Healing and Shamanism* (New York: Fireside/Simon & Schuster, 1987), p. 198.

14. Klimo, op. cit., pp. 61-64, 67; George W. Meek (ed.), *Healers and the Healing Process* (Wheaton, IL: Theosophical Publishing/Quest Book, 1977), pp. 13-70.

15. Walter Martin, *The Kingdom of the Cults* (Minneapolis, MN: Bethany, 1985), rev., p. 227. Martin estimates over 4 million spiritists in South America.

16. Vaz, op. cit., p. 27.

17. Klimo, op. cit., p. 45.
18. Ibid., pp. 43-44
19. Ibid., pp. 48-49.
20. According to Merv Griffin, The Merv Griffin Show, July 25, 1986.
21. Klimo, op. cit., p. 49.
22. Erika Bourguignon, (ed.), Religion, Altered States of Consciousness and Social Change (Columbia: Ohio State University Press, 1973), pp. 16-17; Table 2.
23. Orthodox Christianity and Judaism are almost alone in the universal condemnation of seeking to contact the spirit world. The practice is accepted, variously, among Hindus, Buddhists, Sufis, Sikhs, Muslims, Kabbalists, Taoists, Animists, etc. See the extensive discussion in James Hastings (ed.), Encyclopedia of Religion and Ethics (New York: Charles Scribner's Sons, n.d.), Vol. 4, pp. 565-636.
24. This is proven beyond reasonable doubt by both the history of the occult and the modern data from parapsychology. See e.g., Douglas, op. cit., pp. 87-360; Gauld, op. cit., pp. 153-364; Naomi Hintze and Gaither Pratt, The Psychic Realm, What Can You Believe? (New York: Random House, 1975), pp. 135-223; Norma Bowles and Fran Hynds, Psi-search (San Francisco: Harper & Row, 1978), pp. 51-91.
25. John Warwick Montgomery, (ed.), Demon Possession: A Medical, Historical, Anthropological and Theological Symposium (Minneapolis, MN: Bethany Fellowship, 1976); Malachi Martin, Hostage to the Devil: The Possession and Exorcism of Five Living Americans (New York: Bantam, 1977); William M. Alexander, Demonic Possession in the New Testament: Its Historical, Medical and Theological Aspects (Grand Rapids, MI: Baker, 1980); John L. Nevius, Demon Possession (Grand Rapids, MI: Kregel, 1970).
26. Satprem, Sri Aurobindo or the Adventure of Consciousness (New York: Harper & Row, 1974), p. 199, c.f., 197, 201.
27. Robert Monroe, Journeys Out of the Body (Garden City, NY: Anchor Books, 1973), pp. 138-139.
28. Samuel M. Warren, A Compendium of the Theological Writings of Emanuel Swedenborg (New York: Swedenborg Foundation, 1977), p. 618. See Slater Brown, op. cit., p. 63.
29. Emanuel Swedenborg, The True Christian Religion (New York: E. P. Dutton, 1936), pp. 667-669; Emanuel Swedenborg, Heaven and Its Wonders and Hell (New York: Swedenborg Foundation, 1940), pp. 265-268; Rev. John Whitehead, Posthumous Theological Works of Emanuel Swedenborg, Vol. 1 (New York: Swedenborg Foundation, 1969), p. 452; Samuel M. Warren, A Compendium of the Theological Writings of Emanuel Swedenborg (New York: Swedenborg Foundation, 1977), pp. 376-377.
29a. e.g., Nevius, op. cit., p. 322; chs. 2, 8-10, 14-18.
30. Note the descriptions in Jane Roberts, Seth Speaks (Englewood Cliffs, NJ: Prentice Hall, 1972), pp. 1-2 and back cover photographs; Klimo, op. cit., p. 1, 185.
31. e.g., guru Sri Chinmoy has produced thousands of paintings by automatic painting. In less than two hours on June 26, 1975 Sri Chinmoy painted 500 paintings. Sri Chinmoy (Jamaica, NY: Aum Publications, n.d.), pp. 15-18; Rosemary Brown, Unfinished Symphonies (New York: William Morrow & Company, 1971); Medium Rosemary Brown has composed hundreds of musical pieces in styles very similar to the famous dead composers she claims work through her.
32. Klimo, op. cit., pp. 185-186; Raphael Gasson, The Challenging Counterfeit (Plainfield, NJ: Logos, 1970), pp. 83, 87.
33. Klimo, op. cit., ch. 6 discusses many of these forms.
34. Clifford Wilson and John Weldon, Psychic Forces and Occult Shock (Greenville, NC: Global Publishers, 1987), pp. 282-283.
35. Klimo, op. cit., pp. 46-47, 50, 61, 64; Edward Rosenfeld, The Book of Highs: 250 Ways to Alter Consciousness Without Drugs (New York: Quadrangle/The New York Times Book Company, 1973).
36. Edmond C. Gruss, The Ouija Board: Doorway to the Occult (Chicago: Moody Press, 1975); Stoker Hunt, Ouija: The Most Dangerous Game (New York: Perennial/ Harper & Row, 1985).
37. Gasson, op. cit., ch. 1; Victor Ernest, I Talked with Spirits (Wheaton, IL: Tyndale House, 1971), ch. 1.
38. Klimo, op. cit., p. 3.
39. Ibid., p. 1; Ankerberg and Weldon, op. cit., pp. 15-16.
40. Ibid., pp. 5, 18, 168-184; Elliott Miller, "Channeling—Spiritistic Revelations for the New Age" (Part One), Christian Research Journal, Fall 1987, p. 14.
41. Pat Rodegast and Judith Stanton, Emmanuel's Book: A Manual for Living Comfortably in the Cosmos (New York: Some Friends of Emmanuel, 1985), p. XXI.
42. e.g., Klimo, op. cit., pp. 14, 20, 39, 131-132, 205-320; see Wilson and Weldon, Psychic Forces, op. cit., Part 3.
43. C. S. Lewis, The Screwtape Letters (New York: MacMillan, 1943, 1969), pp. 32-33.
44. e.g., Klimo, op. cit., pp. 39, 131-132, 184, 237-253.
45. Ibid., pp. 183-184.
46. Another analysis will be found in Miller, op. cit., Part 2.
47. Martin Ebon observes, "The mesmeric, or hypnotic, trance bears a close resemblance to the mediumistic trance." Martin Ebon, "History of Parapsychology" in

Martin Ebon (ed.), *The Signet Handbook of Parapsychology* (New York: Signet, 1978), p. 24. Edgar Cayce became a medium through hypnosis. See Thomas Sugrue, *There is a River* (New York: Holt, Rinehart and Winston, 1942); Alan Spraggett, *Ross Peterson: The New Edgar Cayce* (Garden City, NY: Doubleday, 1977), pp. 14-15; see also Simeon Edmunds, *Hypnotism and ESP* (Los Angeles: Wilshire Books, 1969), pp. 61-155; Simeon Edmunds, *Hypnosis: Key to Psychic Powers* (New York: Samuel Weiser, 1968), pp. 9-63; Eric J. Dingwall (ed.), *Abnormal Hypnotic Phenomena: A Survey of 19th Century Cases*, Vol. 4 (New York: Barnes and Noble, 1967).

48. Edmunds, op. cit.; Frank Podmore, *Mediums of the 19th Century* (New Hyde Park, NY: University Books, 1963), Vols. 1 and 2; Leslie Shepard, *Encyclopedia of Occultism and Parapsychology* (Detroit, MI: Gale Research Company, 1979), article under "Hypnosis"; Hiroshi Motoyama, *Hypnosis and Religious Superconsciousness* (Tokyo, Japan: The Institute of Religious Psychology, 1971).

49. In fact spirit incorporation resembles a state of deep hypnosis. See Albert Villoldo and Stanley Krippner, *Healing States: A Journey Into the World of Spiritual Healing and Shamanism* (New York: Simon and Schuster, 1987), pp. 197-198; c.f., Klimo, op. cit., pp. 38, 219-227.

50. The Troops for Truddi Chase (Introduction and Epilogue by Robert A. Phillips, Jr.); *When Rabbit Howls* (New York: E. P. Dutton, 1987), pp. xvii, xxiii, 387-393, 411-415. See note 52.

51. Villoldo and Krippner, op. cit., pp. 20-21, 38, 197; Klimo, op. cit., pp. 237-247.

52. e.g., Robert A. Phillips, note 50, op. cit., p. X, observes: "Dr. [Frank] Putnam has discovered [in observing over 200 cases] that there are significant differences in brain wave patterns, voice tone and inflection, eye responses to stimuli and other responses to both physical and psychological stimuli among the personalities even though they are found in the same body. My own clinical observation has noted differences in handwriting, syntax, voice, accent, facial appearance, and body stance . . . . The growing body of data indicates that the personalities (or "persons" as some multiples prefer to call them) are quite different and in fact are unique individuals."

53. Kenneth Ring, *Heading Toward Omega: In Search of the Meaning of the Near-Death Experience* (New York: Quill/William Morrow, 1985), esp. chs. 3-9. John Weldon and Zola Levitt, *Is There Life After Death?* (Eugene, OR: Harvest House, 1977); *Anabiosis: The Journal of Near-Death Studies*, volumes to the present.

54. Ben G. Hester, *Dowsing: An Expose of Hidden Occult Forces* (Arlington, CA: Ben G. Hester, 4883 Headrick Avenue, Arlington, CA 92505, 1984), rev. 1984, $7.95.

55. Clifford Wilson and John Weldon, *Close Encounters: A Better Explanation* (San Diego: Master Books, 1978).

56. Clifford Wilson and John Weldon, *Psychic Forces and Occult Shock* (Chattanooga, TN: Global Publishers, 1987), pp. 331-454.

57. e.g., Klimo, op. cit., pp. 6-8; John Ferguson, *An Illustrated Encyclopedia of Mysticism and the Mystery Religions* (New York: Seabury, 1977), p. 148.

58. John Weldon and Zola Levitt, *Psychic Healing* (Chicago: Moody Press, 1982); Paul Reisser, Teri Reisser and John Weldon, *New Age Medicine* (Greenville, NC: Global Publishers, 1988).

59. Klimo, op. cit., pp. 242-247.

60. Hans Bender, "Mediumistic Psychoses" in *Telepathy, Clairvoyance, and Psychokinesis* (Munich: Piper Publishers, 1983).

61. Kurt Koch and Alfred Lechler, *Occult Bondage and Deliverance* (Grand Rapids, MI: Kregel, 1970), p. 31; Part 2; Kurt Koch, *Demonology, Past and Present* (Grand Rapids, MI: Kregel, 1973), pp. 41-42.

62. Wilson Van Dusen, *The Presence of Other Worlds* (San Francisco: Harper & Row, 1974), pp. 117-118, 135-137. In this book he correlates the experiences of the powerful medium Emanuel Swedenborg with his own mental patients.

63. Harry Thomsen, *The New Religions of Japan* (Rutland, VT: Charles E. Tuttle, 1971), pp. 15-18. In *Soka Gakkai: Japan's Militant Buddhists* (John Knox, 1968), p. 28, Noah S. Brannen observes that one-third of the popular religions of Japan began from special revelation by a god or spirit being.

63a. Thomsen, op. cit., p. 200.

64. Robert S. Ellwood, Jr., *Religious and Spiritual Groups in Modern America* (Englewood Cliffs, NJ: Prentice Hall, 1973), p. 12 where he states, "The cult phenomena could almost be called a modern resurgence of shamanism." Dr. Weldon's 8 years of research into 65 modern religious cults and sects revealed spiritistic origins or associations in every one.

65. Klimo, op. cit., p. 8; his arguments here concerning Christianity (pp. 85-90) involve a false interpretation of the Bible.

66. These religions accept spiritistic revelations.

67. John Weldon, *The Encyclopedia of Contemporary American Religions, Sects and Cults*, unpublished.

68. Ibid.

69. e.g., ". . . Kal [the devil] is the Jehovah of the Jewish faith and the Father of the Christian teachings . . ."; "Therefore we really see [Jesus] as a son of Kal . . ." Paul

Twitchell, *The Precepts of Eckankar* (Eckankar, ASOST, n.d.), no. 11, p. 6, and his *Letters to a Chela* (Eckankar, ASOST, 1972) first series, No. 3, p. 1. See the analysis in SCP Journal, *Eckankar: A Hard Look at a New Religion* (Berkeley, CA: Spiritual Counterfeits Project), Vol. 3, No. 1, 1979, pp. 26-28. The Radhasoami Sect from which Eckankar was derived has certain teachings in common with the Cathars of the later Middle Ages who also taught the biblical God was the devil. See Williston Walker et. al., *A History of the Christian Church*, 4th ed., 1985, p. 302.

70. David Lane, "Eckankar in Turmoil, Part 1," *Understanding Cults and Spiritual Movements—Research Series*, Vol. 2, No. 1 (Del Mar, CA: Del Mar Press), pp. 1-6, 17-19.

71. SCP Journal, *Eckankar: A Hard Look at a New Religion*, op. cit., pp. 7-22.

72. Ibid., pp. 1-55; Lane, op. cit., pp. 1-6, 17-15.

73. SCP Journal, op. cit., pp. 14-21, 45-47.

74. Ibid., pp. 42-44.

75. Ibid., pp. 24-27.

76. Ibid., pp. 6-22.

77. Ibid., pp. 34-37.

78. Ibid., and Lane, op. cit., Vol. 2, No. 1.

79. SCP Journal, op. cit., p. 39.

80. Klimo, op. cit., p. 297.

81. Ibid.

82. Ibid., p. 296.

83. Colin Wilson, *Mysteries: An Investigation Into the Occult, the Paranormal and the Supernatural* (New York: G. P. Putnam's Sons, 1978), pp. 460, 484.

84. James Hastings (ed.), op. cit., Vol. 4, pp. 565-636.

85. e.g., lifelong occultist David Conway, "A Word About Demons," in his *Magic: An Occult Primer* (New York: Bantam, 1973), pp. 196-199. He discusses how evil the demons are and the damage they can do, noting their chief aim is to destroy men, especially occultists.

86. John Warwick Montgomery, *Demon Possession*, op. cit. (Bethany, 1976); T. K. Oesterreich, *Possession: Demonical and Other* (Citadel, 1974); Malachi Martin, *Hostage to the Devil* (Bantam, 1977); no author, *Demon Experiences in Many Lands—A Compilation* (Chicago: Moody Press, 1960).

87. Doreen Irvine, *Freed from Witchcraft* (Thomas Nelson, 1978), p. 138.

88. M. Scott Peck, *People of the Lie: The Hope for Healing Human Evil* (New York: Simon & Schuster, 1983), p. 190.

88a. See William Lane Craig, *The Son Rises* (Chicago: Moody Press, 1987) for a stalwart historical defense of the resurrection.

89. John Warwick Montgomery, *Principalities and Powers* (Minneapolis, MN: Bethany, 1973), p. 146.

90. John Warwick Montgomery (ed.), *Demon Possession*, op. cit., p. 232.

91. Edmond Gruss, *The Ouija Board: Doorway to the Occult* (Chicago: Moody Press, 1975), pp. 83-94.

92. On human sacrifice see Nigel Davies, *Human Sacrifice in History and Today* (New York: William Morrow, 1981), pp. 13-28, 84-87, 92-98, 275-289; *The Chattanooga Times*, March 25, 1988, where a 7-year-old girl is murdered by a Hindu priest in a ritual offering to a goddess; and Maury Terry, *The Ultimate Evil: An Investigation of America's Most Dangerous Satanic Cult* (Garden City, NY: Doubleday/Dolphin, 1987), introduction, ch. 25; on the Atlanta slayings, Sondra A. O'Neal (Emory University in Atlanta), *King City: Fathers of Anguish, of Blood: The True Story Behind the Atlanta Murders* (unpublished).

93. Robert Somerlott, *Here, Mr. Splitfoot* (New York: Viking, 1971), p. 12; Edmond Gruss, op. cit., recommends Dr. Charles C. Cumberland's *Mexican Revolution: Genesis Under Madero* which identifies Francisco I. Madero, the originator of the Mexican revolution as a leader of spiritism in Mexico. According to a report in the *Wall Street Journal*, June 12, 1987, a similar situation may currently exist in Panama.

94. *Los Angeles Times*, October 4, 1977.

95. Nandor Fodor, op. cit., p. 266; Bhagwan Shree Rajneesh, "Suicide or Sannyas," *Sannyas*, No. 2, 1978, pp. 27-31; Gruss op. cit., p. 75; Martin Ebon (ed.), *The Satan Trap: Dangers of the Occult* (Garden City, NY: Doubleday, 1976), pp. 232-236; Doreen Irvine, *Freed From Witchcraft* (Nashville: Thomas Nelson), p. 121; J. D. Pearce-Higgins, "Dangers of Automatism," *Spiritual Frontiers*, Autumn 1970, p. 216; Morton Kelsey, *The Christian and the Supernatural* (Minneapolis: Augsburg, 1976), p. 41.

96. Elliott O'Donnell, *The Menace of Spiritualism* (New York: Frederick A. Stokes, 1920), p. XII.

97. *Human Behavior*, September 1977, pp. 26-27.

98. J. N. D. Anderson in *The World's Religions* (Grand Rapids, MI: Eerdman's, 1968), p. 55; J. M. Rodwell, trans., *The Koran* (New York: Dutton, 1977), preface, pp. 5, 13-14; William Miller, *A Christian Response to Islam*, NJ: Presbyterian and Reformed, 1977), pp. 19-20; and Sura 32:22, 44:29, in Rodwell text.

99. Thomas Surgrue, op. cit., p. 210.

100. Holistic Life Magazine, Summer 1985, p. 30: For another example, see Laeh Garfield, *Companions in Spirit: A Guide to Working with your Spirit Helpers* (Berkeley, CA: Celestial Arts, 1984), pp. 92-93.

101. Andrija Puharich, *Uri* (New York: Bantam, 1975), pp. 173, 188-189.

102. as told by his friend Colin Wilson, *Mysteries*, op. cit., p. 451.

103. Gasson, op. cit., p. 130.

104. Kurt Koch cites a figure of 9 out of 10 cases of occult involvement harming people, supported by "many thousands of examples." *Occult Bondage and Deliverance*, op. cit., p. 30.

104a. Nandor Fodor, op. cit., pp. 233-238; Gasson, op. cit., p. 87.

105. Dr. Nandor Fodor, op. cit., p. 234 observes: "After prolonged exercise of mediumship intemperance often sets in. The reason is a craving for stimulants following the exhaustion and depletion felt after the seance. Many mediums have been known who succumbed to the craving and died of delirium tremens."; the editors of Psychic Magazine, *Psychics: Indepth Interviews*, pp. 16-17; c.f., Ford's autobiography *Unknown but Known: My Adventure into the Meditative Dimension* (New York: Harper & Row, 1968).

106. Merrill Unger, *The Haunting of Bishop Pike* (Wheaton, IL: Tyndale House, 1971).

107. Keene, op. cit., p. 142.

107a. Fodor, op. cit., mentions cases of mediums who were weighed during ectoplasmic manifestations and lost from 10-118 pounds; the weight of the medium's body apparently decreases proportionately to the spirit's use of the medium's body to produce the materialized "phantom," which, in one case weighed from 52-77 pounds. See Arthur Conan Doyle, *The History of Spiritualism* (New York: Arno, 1975), Vol. 1, p. 278.

108. Joseph Millard, *Edgar Cayce* (Fawcett Gold Metal, 1967), pp. 98, 104-116, 156, 198-201.

109. Keene, op. cit., pp. 133, 140; Fodor, op. cit., p. 234.

110. Keene, op. cit., p. 141, observes "cheating, lying, stealing, conning—these are sanctified in the ethics of mediumship as I knew it."

111. Keene, op. cit., pp. 135, 142; Fodor, op. cit., p. 234; Carl A. Wickland, *30 Years Among the Dead* (Van Nuys, CA: Newcastle, rpt., 1974), p. 154.

112. Wickland, op. cit., pp. 17, 95, 116, 185; Martin Ebon (ed.), *The Satan Trap: Dangers of the Occult* (Garden City, NY: Doubleday, 1976).

113. Keene, op. cit., pp. 147-148.

114. Sri Chinmoy, *Astrology, the Supernatural and the Beyond*, (Jamaica, NY: Angi Press, 1973), p. 62.

115. Kurt Koch, *Occult Bondage and Deliverance*, op. cit., p. 31; Kurt Koch, *Occult ABC* (Germany: Literature Mission Aglasterhausen, Inc.), p. 238.

116. Nandor Fodor, op. cit., p. 235; Hereword Carrington, *Your Psychic Powers and How to Develop Them* (Van Nuys, CA: Newcastle, 1975), p. 62.

117. Fodor, op. cit., p. 235.

118. Malachi Martin, *Hostage to the Devil*, op. cit., p. 419, c.f., 385-488.

119. Ibid., p. 418.

120. Ibid., p. 485.

121. Gasson, op. cit., Ernest, op. cit.